A New True Book

THE CHIPPEWA

By Alice Osinski

The author would like to thank
Raymond Skinaway, State of Minnesota
Indian Affairs Council, for his assistance

CHILDRENS PRESS ®

CHICAGO

Chippewa dancer, Grand Portage
Reservation, Minnesota

For Mary Weasel Bear

PHOTO CREDITS

© Reinhard Brucker—8, 12, 14
(bottom right), 28, 33

Historical Pictures Service,
Chicago—4 (top), 6, 19, 22, 37

Minnesota Historical Society—17, 27

The Newberry Library—21, 34

Northwind Picture Archives—24

© Photri—11, 13, 18 (left)

Root Resources: © John Kohout—
25 (right)
© Kitty Kohout—25 (left)

© John Running Photographs—Cover
2, 4 (bottom), 14 (bottom left), 31,
45 (middle and right)

© Shostal—43 (right)

© Linda Skinaway—40 (2 photos), 41
(2 photos), 43 (left and center),
45 (left)

Smithsonian Institution, National
Anthropological Archives—14 (top),
39 (2 photos)

State Historical Society of
Wisconsin—18 (right)

Cover: Powwow at Grand Portage
Reservation, MN

Library of Congress Cataloging-in-Publication Data

Osinski, Alice.
  Chippewa.

  (A New true book)
  Includes index.
  Summary: Presents a brief history of the Chippewa
Indians describing their customs and traditions and
how they are maintained in the modern world.
    1. Chippewa Indians—Juvenile literature.
[1. Chippewa Indians. 2. Indians of North America]
I. Title.
E99.C6085 1987   977'.00497   86-32687
ISBN 0-516-01230-4

FOURTH PRINTING 1992
Childrens Press, Chicago
Copyright ©1987 by Regensteiner Publishing Enterprises, Inc.
All rights reserved. Published simultaneously in Canada.
Printed in the United States of America.
      7 8 9 10 R 00 99 98 97 96 95 94 93

TABLE OF CONTENTS

In the 1800s George Catlin, famous American artist, made this sketch of Chippewas gathering wild rice. Today, Chippewas gathering wild rice (below) at Leech Lake, Minnesota

PEOPLE OF
THE GREAT LAKES

Slowly, a small canoe
guided by Chippewa
Indians moves through the
tall weeds near the shore
of a shallow lake in
Minnesota. It is the
beginning of the season
for gathering wild rice. The
Chippewa gather rice
much like their ancestors
did hundreds of years ago.
Most Chippewa have

Chippewa camp, from a painting by George Catlin

always lived near woodlands and lakes where fish and game were plentiful. Once small bands of Chippewa lived in Canada, near Sault Sainte Marie. Then about 500 years ago, they joined larger Indian tribes and came west to find better hunting grounds.

Chippewa settled around the Great Lakes.

Some Chippewa stopped at Lake Huron in what is now northern Michigan. Others moved on to the lands around Lake Superior and northern Minnesota. Because the Chippewa traded guns with the fur traders, they forced the Sioux Indians

7

A Chippewa village as it might have looked about 1840

living in the area westward.
By 1840 many Chippewa
were living in Minnesota.
Others had settled in parts
of Canada, Michigan,
Wisconsin, North Dakota,
and Montana.

A WOODLAND
WAY OF LIFE

Except for those living on the plains of North Dakota and Montana most Chippewa made their homes in thickly wooded areas near rivers and lakes. They lived in small family groups, sharing food-gathering places with neighboring Chippewa families.

9

Everything they used came from the forest. Their food, houses, weapons, utensils, clothing, and medicine came from wood, bark, plants, or the animals and birds of the forest.

From young trees Chippewas built dome-shaped houses called wigwams. Men placed the tree poles in the ground and bent them to form

This photograph shows a temporary Chippewa village being built on the shore of Mille Lac in Minnesota. Two small dwellings are partially covered with birchbark.

arches. Women then tied the poles together with basswood strips and covered them with long sheets of tree bark.

Often, pine branches covered the floor of the wigwam. The branches made the ground softer and added a pleasant pine scent to the home.

A wigwam was a good house for a family. It kept them warm in winter when the most time was spent inside. In the spring, when the family needed to move, the bark that

Woman weaving a mat of rush, a grasslike plant
that grows in marshes or damp prairies

covered the wigwam was
simply rolled up and taken
to a new campsite.

When not on a winter
hunt, men repaired or
made traps and useful
wooden items, such as
bowls and spoons. Women
wove fishnets, mats, and

Chippewas decorate their clothing and crafts. The dental pictograph (right), made by biting a design into birch bark, and the beaded shirt and headband (below left) were decorated with flower patterns. Some useful items, like the split wood basket (bottom right), were not decorated.

containers from the bark
of the birch tree.

Sometimes they folded thin
sheets of birchbark in two,
and bit designs into them
with their teeth. Chippewa
women also made clothing
for the family from the
skins of beaver, squirrel,
rabbit, and deer. They
decorated the things they
made with shells, beads,
feathers, and porcupine
quills.

SNOWSHOES AND BIRCHBARK CANOES

Chippewa families moved often throughout the year. The need to travel to seasonal food sources took them from hunting grounds and trapping areas to maple tree groves, berry patches, rice lakes, and fishing sites.

On rivers and lakes Chippewas traveled in

Building a birchbark canoe in 1895

birchbark canoes. Canoes
made of birch were light
but tough. The frame was
made of white cedar. Then
it was covered with strips
of birchbark and sewn
together with special
spruce tree roots that

Sewing tree bark to the canoe frame (top). Young Chippewas hunting deer on snowshoes (right)

would not rot in winter.
The seams were sealed
with spruce or pine gum.
Sleds and snowshoes
were used for winter
travel. Snowshoes looked
like tennis rackets. The

Watercolor made in 1823 of a Chippewa family traveling to a fresh food supply

frame was formed from a thin piece of ash, crisscrossed with strips of moosehide. When Chippewas traveled with heavy loads, they placed the loads on wooden sleds. The sleds were pulled by hand or sometimes by a team of dogs.

SUGAR-MAKING SEASON

In late March or early spring, families moved to maple groves where they collected sap from the trees. Sugar was made from maple sap and was used to season much of their food. It was used also as candy and as a sweet drink.

Sap was collected in birchbark buckets and

Typical Indian sugar camp

poured into containers
made of moosehide.
Women boiled the sap
until it thickened. Then it
was strained and cooked
some more. They worked
the thick syrup into grains
of sugar. More recently,
some maple syrup was

21

poured into molds and made into hard sugar.

The sugar-making season was a happy time for families. After the long, lonely winter, everyone enjoyed sharing news. They danced and played games. Canoe racing, a favorite sport, was great fun.

FISHING AND BERRY PICKING

Late in spring people set up villages along lakes and rivers where fish were plentiful. Although fishing was done year-round, spring was a time when families worked together to catch a large supply.

Both men and women fished. They speared some of the fish. Others were caught in large nets or

Sometimes wooden traps were built across rivers to catch fish coming downstream.

traps. Chippewas living along Lake Ontario caught salmon and sturgeon. Those living further north caught whitefish.

Late spring was a time for berry picking, too. Usually, women and children gathered berries, fruits, and nuts. Juicy cranberries were often eaten fresh.

Blueberries (left) and chokecherries (above) were dried and stored for winter needs.

Raspberries were made into a paste or a tasty pudding.

Fishing and berry picking continued throughout the summer. In some areas each family also had its own summer garden where corn, beans, and squash were planted.

GATHERING WILD RICE

At the beginning of fall Chippewa families divided into small groups and moved to shallow lakes or streams where wild rice grew. For several weeks they collected rice and dried it.

Using long poles, men guided birchbark canoes through the thick rice beds while women knocked the rice kernels into the

Gathering wild rice in 1925

canoe with a pair of cedar
sticks. When the canoe
was full it was returned to
shore. Here the women
built fires. The rice was
dried until the shells fell
away from the kernels. The
rice was then roasted over
a fire. **27**

Each year after the rice crop was harvested the Chippewa held a ceremony to give thanks for the rice that was taken from the lakes. At this time some rice was cooked and eaten. The rest of the rice was stored in containers for later use.

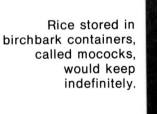

Rice stored in birchbark containers, called mococks, would keep indefinitely.

PRAYING TO THE SPIRITS

Chippewas prayed often throughout each day. They prayed to the Manito-k (spirits) also to Kichi-Manitu (the Great Spirit) who watched over their lives. The spirits were found in water, rocks, trees, stars, weather, and in the four directions (east, west, north, and south). People left small gifts of tobacco for the spirits when they prayed.

Pinches of tobacco were thrown on the water before rice was gathered. Often tobacco was placed below a tree from which medicine was taken. Tobacco was sometimes smoked in pipes along with each prayer. Chippewa believed that smoke from the tobacco carried the words of their prayers to the Kichi-Manitu or the Great Spirit.

Chippewa doctors practiced a form of

Even today, some traditional Chippewa dancers may carry
medicine bags that contain objects to protect them.

medicine called Midéwin
or Great Medicine Dance.
In return for tobacco or
food, the medicine man and
woman healed the sick
and performed special
religious ceremonies. From

the Great Spirit and teachers they learned which plants and roots to give the sick. They also learned the special songs that must be sung while they used their power to heal.

Besides medicine songs, there were also songs to protect hunters and to bring success on the trail. Other songs were sung to bring a good harvest of maple syrup and wild rice.

FUR-TRADING DAYS

After wild rice was harvested in the fall, families moved back to the woods where they began preparing for winter. In November men set out on the winter hunt. They

Spearing muskrats in winter

trapped mink, otter, muskrat, rabbit, fox, and beaver. Larger animals such as deer, bear, moose, and wolves were hunted, too. Chippewas believed bears were sacred or holy animals. Each time a bear was killed, a special ceremony was held to honor it.

The Chippewa believed all animals were like their relatives. They were placed on earth by the Great Spirit to help them survive the long, cold winters and hot summers.

In the 1600s, when non-Indians began trapping on Chippewa land, life changed. Many Chippewas moved farther west, away from the French trappers and fur traders. Others welcomed the French as friends. They let the French live among them. Then the English came. Soon the French and the English had built trading posts and were trading guns, cloth, beads, and blankets with the Indians for furs.

At this time some Chippewas began selling their land. The French, the English, and later the

A painting of a small Chippewa and American community

Americans fought to own the land. The Americans finally won. Slowly, they took over Chippewa country. Although Chippewas fought to keep their land, they lost.

Many agreements, called treaties, were made

between the Chippewa
tribes and the United
States. Each time a treaty
was signed, the Chippewa
had to give up more of
their land. By the 1800s,
the United States
government had placed
Chippewas on reservations
(land intended for Indians).

In 1854 the Lake
Superior band of Chippewa
was moved to a
reservation near Duluth
and Grand Portage,

Early photographs show the changes that were happening in Indian life.

Minnesota. Three years
later, in 1857, the largest
reservation in Minnesota
was created by treaty.
Today it is known as
White Earth. Other
Chippewa reservations can

Ojibway school in Fond du Lac, Minnesota (left), and new housing (right). Chippewas were originally called Ojibways. This name was mispronounced as Chippewas, the name by which they have commonly become known to Americans.

be found in Wisconsin and Canada.

Once on the reservations, Chippewa life changed. They could not hunt or trap as they once did. Indian children were forced to attend schools where they learned to dress, speak, and act as American children.

MODERN LIFE

Today Chippewas live a modern way of life. But they also hold onto the ways of their ancestors. Many Chippewas live on reservations in the United

Selling beadwork at the American Indian Center in Minneapolis (left). A tribal lawyer (below) on the Fond du Lac reservation

States and Canada. Some
still hunt and fish. Each
year families gather berries
and wild rice. They garden
and make maple syrup.

Light industry provides
some jobs on reservations.
There are a few stores,
factories, and lumber mills.
Some Chippewa earn a
living as fishing guides,
teachers, and nurses.
Others work for the tribe
in government jobs.

An Indian leader at Minnesota state capitol (left) tries to pass laws to help all American Indians. A teacher (center) at The Red School House in St. Paul. A fishing guide (right) at White River Reservation, Ontario, Canada.

More than half of the Chippewas have moved away from reservations. They are living in cities such as Chicago, Milwaukee, and Minneapolis. Some have found good jobs there. They work in offices, factories, and at other professional jobs. But many Chippewas cannot get used to city life. Those who cannot get jobs are faced with many problems.

Indian centers in large cities help Chippewas stay in touch with their traditions. They help them deal with problems of city living.

Whether in cities or on reservations, Chippewas know how important it is to hold on to their special way of life. If they do not

pass on their traditions to their young, those traditions will be lost. Modern Native Americans will never know the beauty of a traditional way of life. Chippewa traditions are more special today than ever before.

WORDS YOU SHOULD KNOW

ancestors(AN • sess • terz) — family members who lived before one's own birth

ash(ASH) — tree whose wood is tough, straight, though elastic; ideal for making frames for snowshoes and other sturdy items

bark(BARK) — rough outer covering of tree trunks and limbs

birchbark(BERCH • bark) — the smooth outer covering of birch trees, which can be separated into paper-thin sheets

Canada(KAN • ah • dah) — country north of the United States

canoe(KAH • noo) — long, narrow boat pointed at the ends, made with a lightweight frame covered with birchbark, animal skins, or hides

ceremony(SAIR • ih • moh • nee) — a set way of celebrating an important occasion

fishnets(FISH • nehtz) — loosely knotted, tied, or woven, mesh-like material to be dropped into water to gather up fish

forest(FOR • ist) — a large area covered with trees and other plant life; also called woods

fur traders(FER TRAY • derz) — men who bought furs from trappers or hunters and sold them to craftsmen and dealers in fur garments, rugs, and the like

game(GAYME) — wild animals, birds, or fish sought by hunters, trappers, fishermen and used as food

gathering(GATHE • er • ing) — to bring together into one place, to collect

Great Lakes(GRATE LAYKES) — five large connected lakes between the United States and Canada

guide(GYDE) — a person who helps another to find or reach a location

harvest(HAR • vist) — to gather, collect grain or crops that are full-grown

hunting grounds(HUN • ting GROUNDZ) — areas where animals and birds are plentiful; good locations to find food both for the wildlife and for the hunter

kernels(KER • nilz) — the soft center part of a seed inside a harder cover

lumber(LUM • ber) — tree logs, or timber, cut into boards, planks

lumber mill(LUM • ber MIHL) — a building or field area where machinery cuts and prepares logs in various sizes and forms

medicine man or woman — native doctor believed by North American Indians to have powers to cure the sick, to make predictions, to call upon heavenly spirits

porcupine quills(POR • kyoo • pine KWILZ) — the needle-sharp pointed spines covering the animal's body

professional(pro • FESH • un • ul) — having great skill, experience or training in a particular activity or employment

rice lakes(RYCE LAYKES) — bodies of water where rice grass shoots grow

snowshoes(SNO • shooz) — tennis-racket-shaped frames woven with thin leather strips, fastened to shoes or boots, allowing easier travel over deep snow

store(STORE) — to put away, to keep for use at a future time

trading posts(TRAY • ding POHSTS) — stores in areas where few people have settled, in which handcrafted goods, fish, animal skins, and the like may be traded for food, clothing, or other items people wish to purchase

traditions(tra • DISH • unz) — rules, practices, behavior, as handed down from generation to generation

tribe(TRYBE) — a large group of persons joined together by common backgrounds, interest, or culture

village(VIL • ij) — an area of dwellings, smaller than a town

weapon(WEP • un) — any item used to fight with

INDEX

About the Author

*Alice Osinski has had a varied career in the field of education. Her
accomplishments include teacher consultant, director of bicultural
curriculum and alternative education programs, and producer of
educational filmstrips. A seven year teaching experience with the
Oglala Sioux of Pine Ridge, SD and Pueblo and Navajo of Gallup,
NM helped to launch her career in writing. Ms. Osinski has written
several articles about the unique life style of American Indians. Her
previous books in the True book series include The Sioux, The
Navajo, and The Eskimo.*